# How to use thes

## Guided Reading

### Walkthrough/Book introduction (pages 2–5)

A *walkthrough* or book introduction is a way of introducing the book to a group of children. It provides an opportunity to introduce children to some of the ideas and words they will meet when they read the book.

Go through the whole book in the walkthrough, before children start reading independently. The walkthrough notes on pages 2 to 5 of this booklet provide prompts for you to use. These will alert children to the ideas and vocabulary they will need when they come to read the book for themselves.

### Independent Reading (pages 2–5)

After doing a walkthrough of the whole book, ask the children to read the text aloud, on their own, at their own pace. Observe each child, praising successful strategies and expressive reading.

The Independent Reading notes on pages 2 to 5 of this booklet offer suggestions for prompting children to check, correct and confirm their own reading.

### After Independent Reading/Returning to the text (page 6)

After the children have read the book independently, return to the text as a group, to reinforce teaching points and check children's understanding. On page 6 there are quick follow-up ideas for related text, sentence and word level work.

### Responding to the text (pages 6–8)

It is important to encourage children to give a personal response to the text. Discussion ideas related to the book are given on page 6.

These Teaching Notes also contain group activity ideas on page 7 and a Photocopy Master on page 8, for use after the guided reading session or in a follow-up literacy session.

# Guided Reading Notes

## Walkthrough *(front and back cover)*

Briefly discuss the types of clothing the children might wear in different weathers. Tell the children this book is about a girl who is telling us what she wears on different days in different weathers.

Read the title and the back cover blurb to the children.

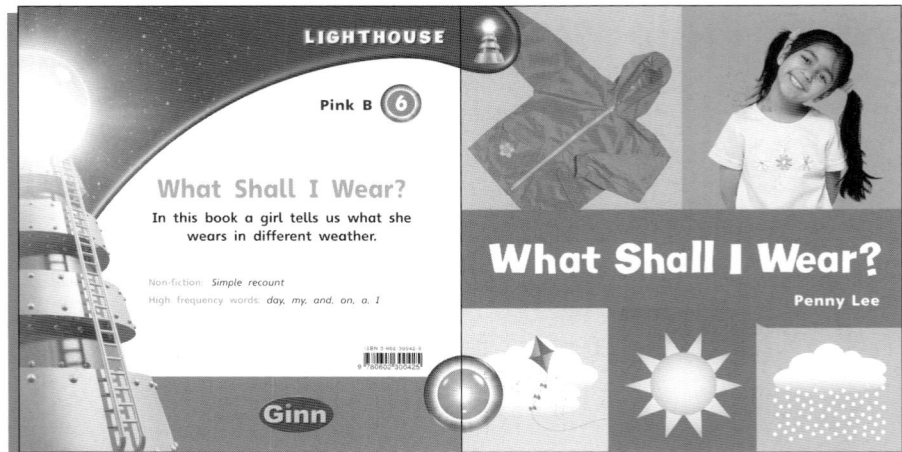

## Walkthrough *(title page)*

**PROMPTS** Let's read the title together. Let me see you pointing to the words to see if they match what you say.

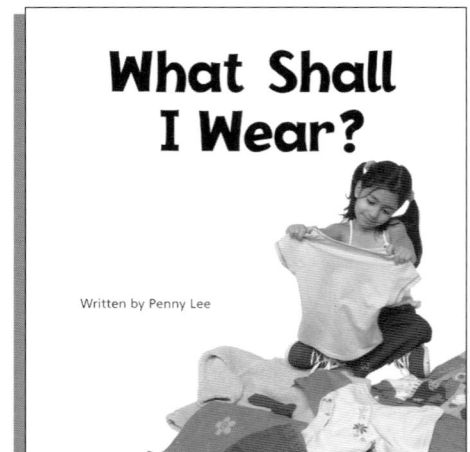

## Independent Reading *(title page)*

**CHECK** that the child is using one-to one-correspondence.

"Good reading. I can see you pointing carefully. Did the words fit what you said?"

## Walkthrough (pages 2–3)

**PROMPTS** Look, it's a sunny day. What does the girl say she wears on a sunny day? Yes, she says, *On a sunny day I wear my T-shirt*.

On a sunny day

I wear my T-shirt.

2

3

## Independent Reading (pages 2–3)

**CHECK** that the child is using picture cues.

"Well done. I can see you looking at the picture to see what the weather's like, and I could see you looking at her T-shirt. Can you see the letter *T* in *T-shirt*?"

## Walkthrough (pages 4–5)

**PROMPTS** On a cloudy day she says she wears her T-shirt and something else. What else can you see? (Prompt for *jumper*.) Yes, she says, *On a cloudy day I wear my T-shirt and my jumper*.

On a cloudy day

I wear my T-shirt

and my jumper.

4

5

## Independent Reading (pages 4–5)

**CHECK** for accurate reading of the words *T-shirt, and,* and *jumper*.

"I liked the way you read *T-shirt* first and you saw what came next. You saw the little word *and*."

If the child says *sweater* instead of *jumper* … "It could be but look at the first letter and think about what that word might be."

## Walkthrough (pages 6–7)

**PROMPTS** What kind of day is this? Yes, it's a rainy day. She wears something else as well as her T-shirt and her jumper. What else does she wear? (Prompt for *coat*.)

On a rainy day

I wear my T-shirt

and my jumper

and my coat.

6

7

## Independent Reading (pages 6–7)

**CHECK** for accurate reading of *and my ... and my ...*

"Did your pointing fit? Well done" *or* "Did your reading match? Let's try again. Read it slowly and we'll check the words as you read them."

## Walkthrough (pages 8–9)

**PROMPTS** What's the weather like here? (Prompt for *windy*.) On a windy day she wears even more clothes. She wears her T-shirt and her jumper and her coat and what else can you see? (Prompt for *scarf*.) Yes, and her scarf.

On a windy day

I wear my T-shirt

and my jumper

and my coat

and my scarf.

8

9

## Independent Reading (pages 8–9)

**CHECK** for one to one correspondence and confident, fluent reading.

"I liked the way you read that as if you were talking. I saw you checking the pictures first with your eyes" *or* "You read all those words beautifully. Now you know what it says, put your hands in your lap and let your eyes do the pointing, then it will sound just like talking."

## Walkthrough (pages 10–11)

**PROMPTS** Can you see what she's added today? (Prompt for *gloves*.) What does she say she wears on a snowy day? She says, *I wear my T-shirt and my jumper and my coat and my scarf and my gloves*.

On a snowy day

I wear my T-shirt

and my jumper

and my coat

and my scarf

and my gloves.

10

11

## Independent Reading (pages 10–11)

**CHECK** that the child is using initial sound clues and cross-checking with picture clues.

"Well done. How did you know that said *scarf*?" (Prompt for memory, first letter and picture cues.)

## Walkthrough (page 12)

**PROMPTS** Now we can see her dressed in all the different kinds of weathers. Let's read them together: *sunny, cloudy, rainy, windy, snowy*.

Sunny

Cloudy

Rainy

Windy

Snowy

12

## Independent Reading (page 12)

**CHECK** that the child notices the difference in the page layout.

"Is this page like the others? How are we going to read it?" (Prompt for reading the words from top left to right, middle and then bottom left to right.)

### Word knowledge – *y* endings

Ask the children to turn to page 6. Ask them to point to the word *rainy*. Ask them to cover up the last letter *y* with a finger. Do they know what the remaining word says? (Prompt for *rain*.) Model this on a board by writing the whole word and rubbing off the y or make the word using magnetic letters and move the y to one side. Repeat the activity with the words *cloudy/windy/snowy*. (The word *sunny* should not be used because of the irregularity of the word when *y* is added.)

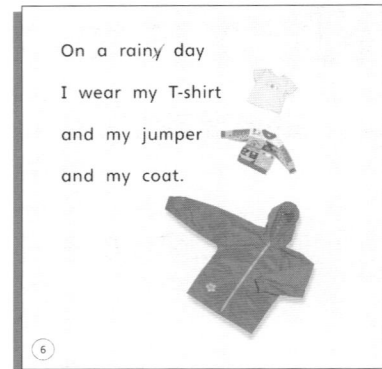

On a rainy day
I wear my T-shirt
and my jumper
and my coat.

6

### Sentence knowledge – match upper and lower case letters

Ask the children to turn to page 12 and to read the labels for the pictures. Discuss how capital letters have been used for the labels. Ask the children to find the matching lower case letter for each capital letter inside the book. Can they write these on the board?

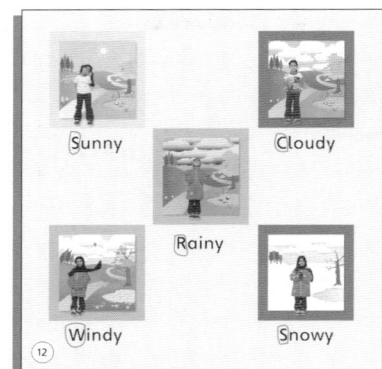

Sunny    Cloudy

Rainy

Windy    Snowy

12

### Text knowledge – non-fiction features

Ask the children if they think this text is a story. Explain that it is a non-fiction book and discuss the basic features of a non-fiction book, e.g. the use of photographs, facts or real events rather than a made-up story, use of labels, etc. Go through the book with the children, looking at these features.

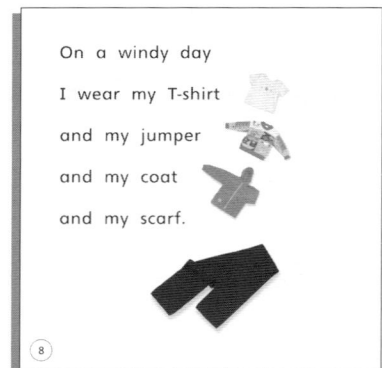

On a windy day
I wear my T-shirt
and my jumper
and my coat
and my scarf.

8

## Responding to the text

- Briefly ask the children to remember which clothing the girl wore on each type of day.

- What activities do they do when it is sunny, cloudy, rainy, windy or snowy? What type of clothing would they wear in each weather?

# **①** *W* is for windy

**AIM** to listen carefully to the initial sounds and match them with the written form (NLS: YR W2)

**YOU WILL NEED**
● pictures from a magazine or hand drawn pictures each showing a different kind of weather from the book, i.e. sunny, cloudy, windy, rainy, snowy

● individual letters cards showing the following letters: *c/r/w/n/s/s*

**WHAT TO DO** Show each picture to the children and ask them to say the type of weather shown. Call out each weather word (leaving *snowy* and *sunny* till last). Get the children in turn to choose a letter card that matches the first sound of the weather word, e.g. *c* for *cloudy*. They then place the letter card on top of the picture. After looking at *windy*, *rainy* and *cloudy*, there will be two *s* cards and the *n* card left. Tell the children that all the cards have to be used up and they may have to listen to the next sound in each weather word. Say the words *sunny* and *snowy* aloud so they can hear the *n* sound in *snowy*. If necessary, write *snowy* on the board so that the children can understand why the *n* card belongs to the snowy picture.

# **②** Weather pot

**AIM** to reinforce reading of words from the book (NLS: YR W5)

**YOU WILL NEED**
● weather words (from the book) written on individual cards

● blu-tack

● five or more small sticks (length of a pencil)

● two small balls of modelling clay

● one or two decorative terracotta pots

**WHAT TO DO** Place each ball of modelling clay on the bottom of each pot to fill its hole. Secure each weather card to the end of a small stick with the blu-tack. Poke the other end of the 'weather stick' into one of the pots making sure it is secure in the modelling clay. Use this as a daily 'weather' activity so the children take it in turns to select the right stick and put it in the empty pot. This could be supplemented with different weather words, (e.g. *frosty/misty*, etc) as the children's vocabulary grows. The other pot could show labels of the days of the week.

On a party day

I wear my _____

and my _____

and _____ _____ .

Ask the children to think of three favourite items of clothing they would love to wear to their birthday party. Ask them to fill in the sentence. (You may need to model the writing and scribe the items of clothing for the children.) The children can then draw themselves in their party clothes in the space above.

**What Shall I Wear?**                    *(NLS: YR T11)*